For Michael, Katie, and Allison

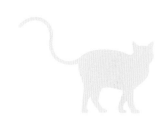

First published in the United States by Peter Pauper Press, Inc.
Originally published in France as *ABC Animaux Animals* by Ah! Agathe Hennig livres jeunesse.
Copyright © Ah! Agathe Hennig livres jeunesse, 2016
English translation copyright © 2020 by Peter Pauper Press, Inc.

Published by Peter Pauper Press, Inc.
202 Mamaroneck Avenue
White Plains, New York 10601 USA

Library of Control Number: 2020934667

ISBN 978-1-4413-3463-3
Manufactured for Peter Pauper Press, Inc.
Printed in Hong Kong

7 6 5 4 3 2 1

Visit us at www.peterpauper.com

ABC
ANIMALS

CHRISTOPHER EVANS

Peter Pauper Press, Inc.
WHITE PLAINS, NEW YORK

Aa Aa

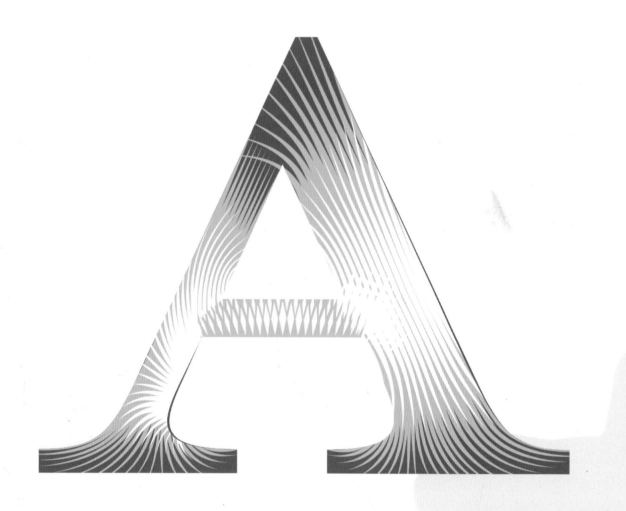

Alpaca

Bb Bb

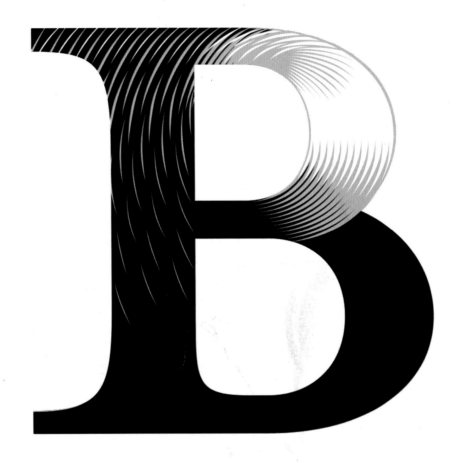

Badger

Cc   Cc

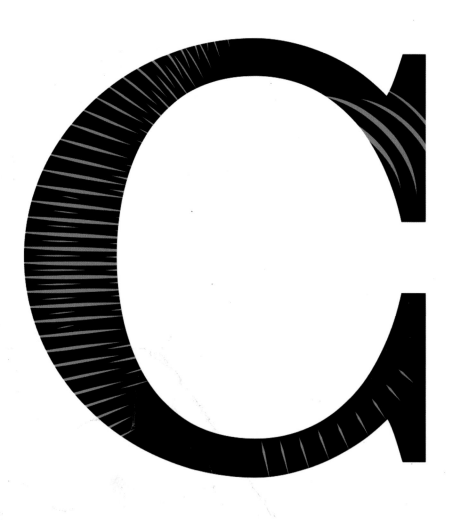

Cat

Dd

Dd

Dolphin

Ee Ɛe

Elephant

Ff Ff

Flamingo

Gg   Gg

Giraffe

Hh

Hedgehog

Ii   Ii

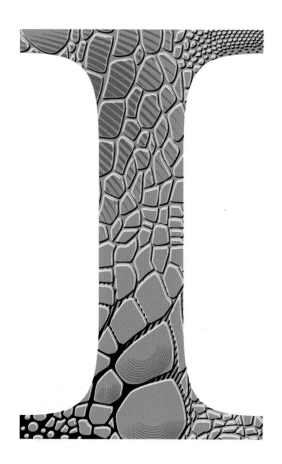

Iguana

Jj

Jj

Jaguar

Kk

Kk

Koala

Ll

Le

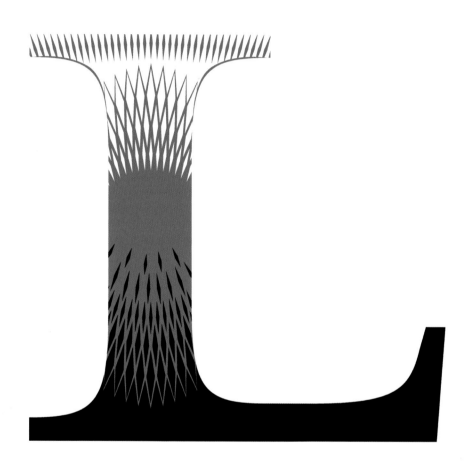

Lemur

Mm

Mm

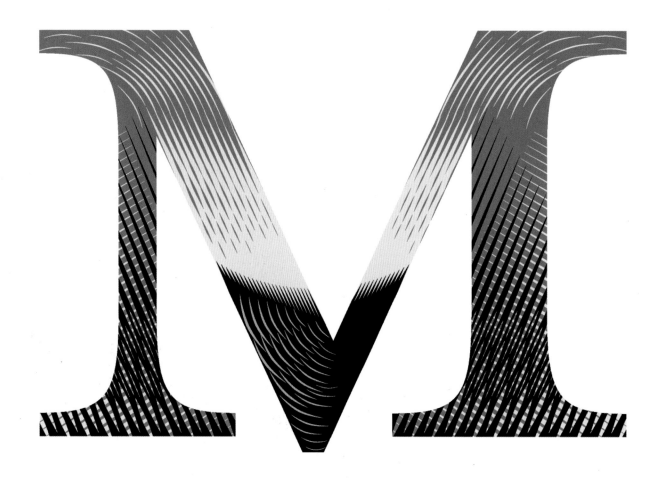

Monkey

N n

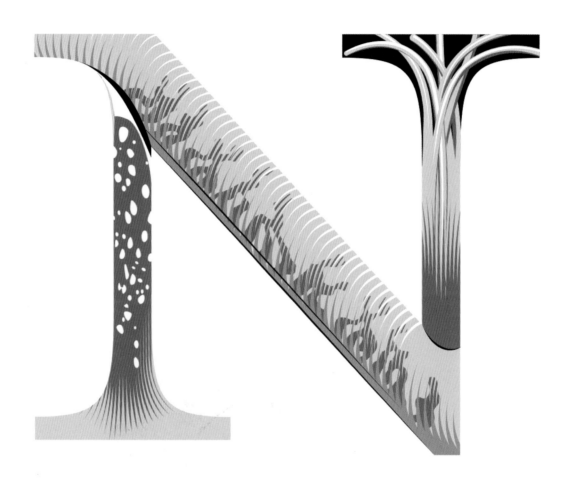

Nautilus

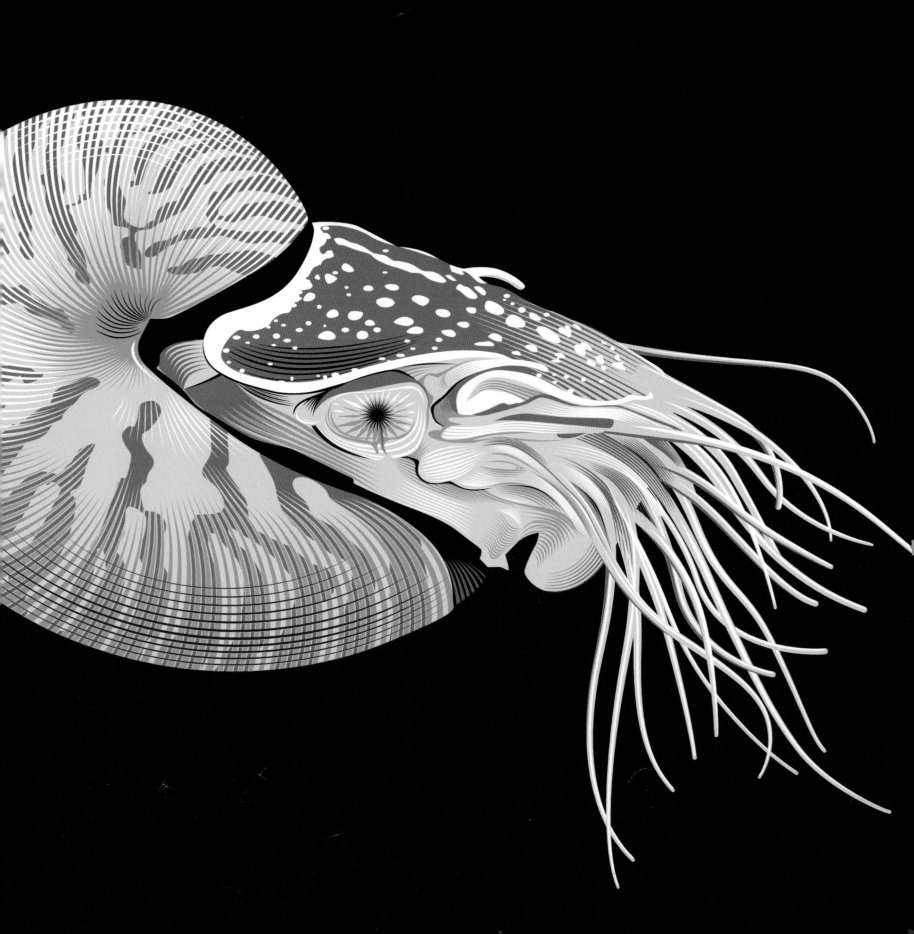

Oo

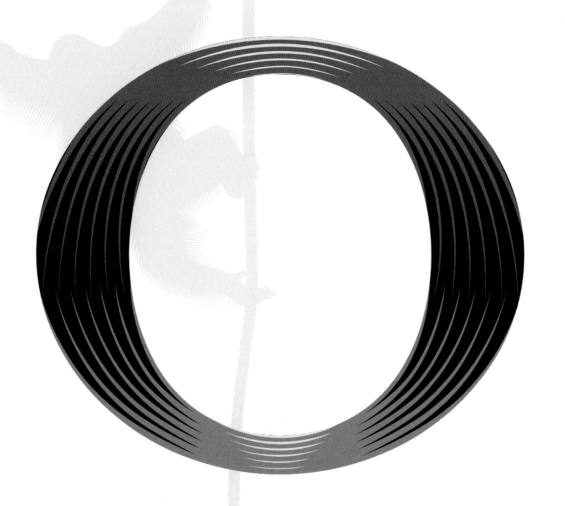

Orangutan

Oo

P p

P p

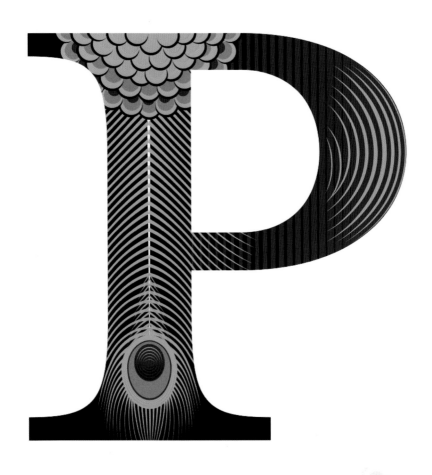

Peacock

Qq   Qq

Quetzal

Rr Rr

Robin

Ss　　　　　　　Ss

Snake

T t   T t

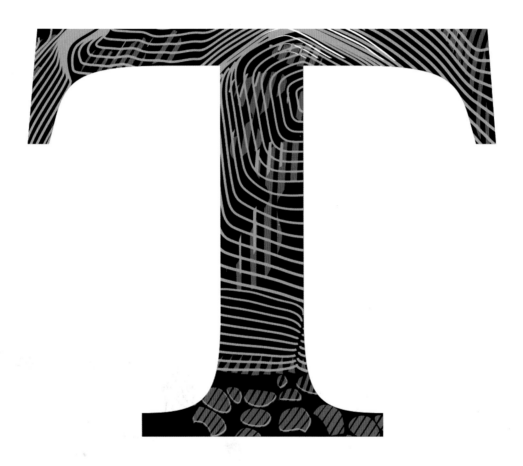

Turtle

Uu Uu

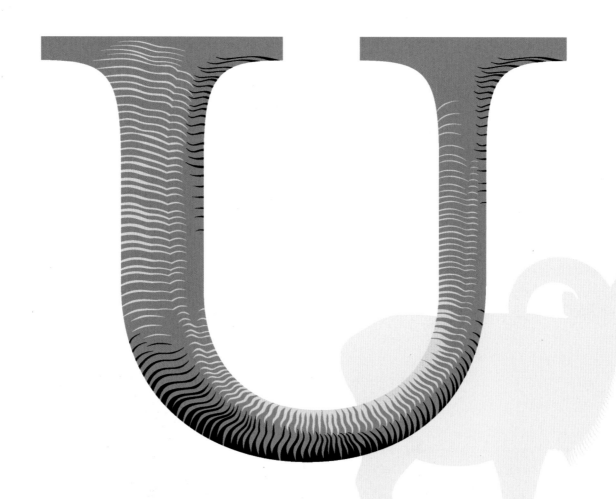

Urial

V v

V υ

Vulture

Ww

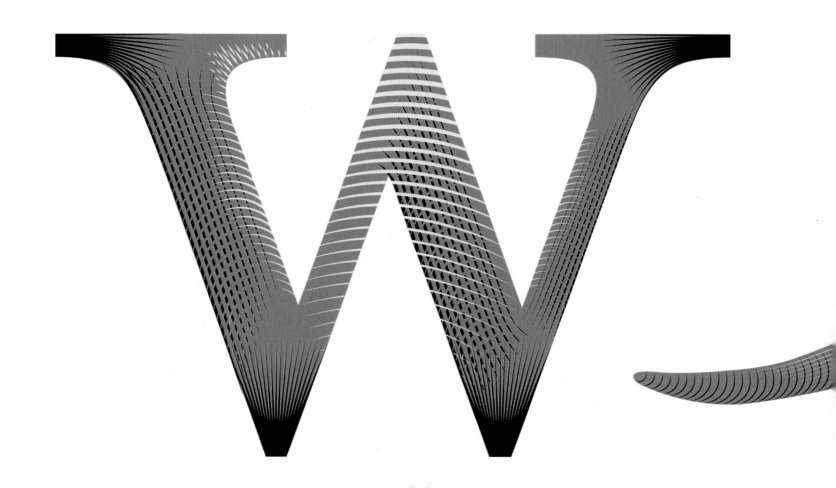

Wallaby

Xx Xx

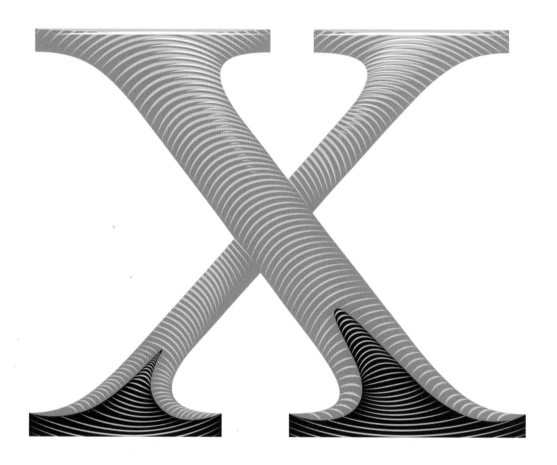

Xenopus

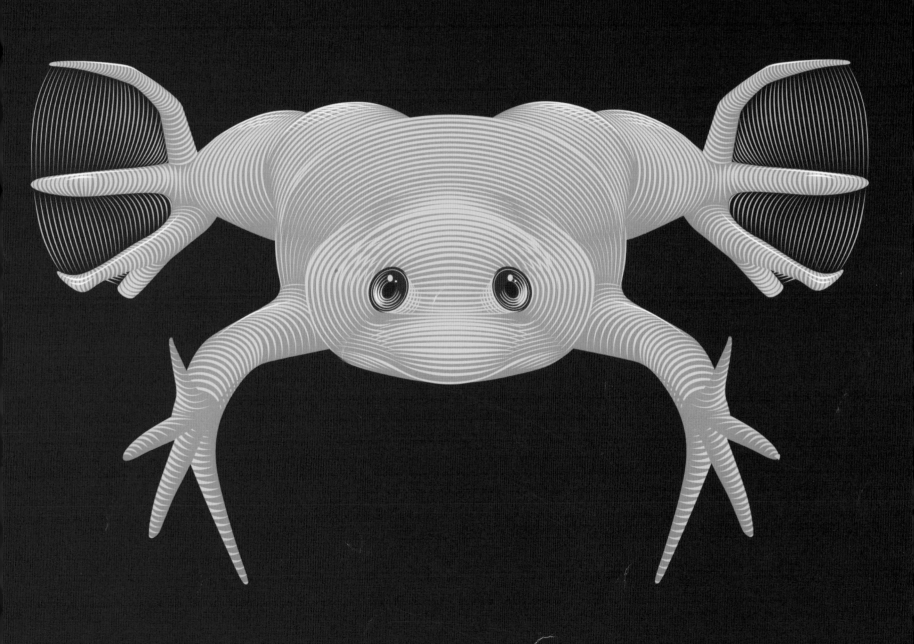

Y y

𝒴 𝓎

Yak

Zz   Zz

Zebra